Should I Wear Floral?

And other poems on Life, Love and Leaving

by

Di Castle

illustrated by Denise A Horn

Matador
9 Priory Business Park,
Wistow Road, Kibworth Beauchamp,
Leicestershire. LE8 0RX
Tel: 0116 279 2299
Email: books@troubador.co.uk
Web: www.troubador.co.uk/matador
Twitter: @matadorbooks

ISBN 978 1788036 559

British Library Cataloguing in Publication Data.
A catalogue record for this book is available from the British Library.

Printed and bound in the UK by TJ International, Padstow, Cornwall
Typeset in 11pt Aldine401 BT by Troubador Publishing Ltd, Leicester, UK

Matador is an imprint of Troubador Publishing Ltd

MIX
Paper from
responsible sources
FSC® C013056

For regular updates from Di Castle, like her facebook page:
https://www.facebook.com/pages/Di-Castle-Writer/266866193324409

She is also on Twitter:
@dinahcas

*In fond memory of my dear friend Jill who would be laughing
out loud, as that is what she did best.*

Life is just one damned thing after another
Elbert Hubbard but sometimes attributed to Frank Ward
O'Malley

Life is the funny thing that happens to you
on the way to the grave
Quentin Crisp

Love conquers all things – except poverty and toothache
Mae West

In this world nothing can be said to be certain,
except death and taxes
Benjamin Franklin

He taught me housekeeping: when I divorce I keep the house
Zsa Zsa Gabor

Hell is other people
John Paul Sartre

Contents

Preface

After the success of *Grandma's Poetry Book*, I transferred the document to the external hard drive and then found more humorous poems remained. Written over the last thirty years they form a social commentary on our society as well as my own life.

I am often asked where the poems come from and sometimes I am hard-pressed to answer. Most poems in *Should I Wear Floral?* are a reaction to national events, stages of life, or offer a window on what can, at times, be a very strange world. A phrase or line repeats itself over and over in my head. The first words of 'What Happened?' flew into my mind when I was at the local tip and saw a black bag overflowing with Christmas decorations, unwritten cards and other seasonal detritus. It was apparent the bag's contents were from an elderly person's home. The sadness I felt seeing personal items so unceremoniously dumped prompted the idea that Christmas would not be coming round again for this person.

My wedding verse was prompted by a trip to the West End for my daughter's 18th birthday, some thirty years or more ago – the show, Kiss Me Kate. One song is a clever play on words – Brush Up Your Shakespeare. Despite my teaching career, personal speeches fill me with dread and to recite a verse was easier. There is more truth in the 'Wedding Verse' than listeners and readers might think.

Many poems originate with news stories. 'Why can't I go… to that place' refers to a deaf girl, with several A grade A Levels, refused admission to a prestigious university. At the time, despite equal opportunities legislation, there was poor provision for deaf students. I am delighted that this debacle would not be repeated at the time of writing this preface in 2016. My knowledge of the Deaf – my sister is profoundly deaf – inspired the verse.

September Daze was written two months after my move to Swanage when emails from ex-colleagues brought news of the stresses and strains of a new academic year. I am sure teachers will identify with the sentiments. In fact, during final proofreading, a video circulated on Facebook showed teachers on an inset day singing 'One More Day', a parody on the song from Les Miserables. Perfect!

'Fat Chances' was prompted by the burgeoning obesity problems in the early years of the new millennium and, even now, this shows no signs of abating. The poem, 2003, was inspired by news stories around the end of 2002 and the New Year. Even I can't remember all the news items but England was clearly not doing too well on the cricket pitch! It was written before the invasion of Iraq and so this is not mentioned, save for hints of events behind closed doors.

I have always written verse for family birthdays,

weddings and other events. 'A Simple Life' was written in 2002 on the death of my mother-in-law. My own mother died when I was 23, so Eva became a surrogate Mum to me and a valued part of my life. She certainly led a simple, uncomplicated life, advising me often to 'do less' when overcome by life and work commitments. She was convinced I would get published eventually so this poem is a tribute to her.

'The Boomerang Generation' was a term used in 2001 for the growing trend for post-graduate or working youngsters to return home to live, as soaring house prices and lack of affordable rental property played havoc with their finances and accommodation. I wrote the poem in response to an email from my friend Helen.

I have also included a guest poem from Helen. She and I had great fun working on the Family Literacy Project in Slough before the new millennium. We still wish we had published something akin to our email exchanges as we prepared our sessions. We share a great sense of humour. Her Christmas 2015 poem on new words amused me and it arrived just as this book was nearing completion.

The 'Look Down Generation' was a phrase coined in 2015 in a national newspaper, to describe people of all ages who spend more time looking down at phones and ipads than talking to each other.

Some of life's irritations are made more bearable by putting ideas into print. This was the case with 'Excuse Me If I Smash Your Phone'. Travelling long distances by train in carriages where phones are not banned can become fractious. Even in the 'silent' carriages people do not switch off.

My illustrator, Denise, captures the essence of all my poems, which is why, I believe, we have such a fantastic working and personal relationship. She can 'see' the line to accentuate and her illustrations always amaze. Our previous book, *Grandma's Poetry Book*, was well received with reviews likening her work to that of EH Sheppard of the A A Milne books. I was – and still am – a huge fan of When We Were Young and Now We Are Six. When I give talks to groups, I begin by reading The Four Friends which was a childhood favourite.

The poem, 'Should I Wear Floral?', was the catalyst for this book. As a writer and frequent rail traveller, I observe people, eavesdropping conversations – a constant source of irritation to my long-suffering partner. One day returning from the outer reaches of Brighton to the main station I became aware of four women, all dressed differently, but with one common theme. They all wore floral blouses.

Once on the Southampton train, I penned the poem and on my arrival home sent it to Denise. We decided this could be a good title for the next book. Poems on life, observations, amusing happenings and irritations. I already had poems on love and some on divorce, moving home and bereavement. I immediately thought of the three words: Life, Love and Leaving.

I do hope you enjoy our second book and continue to spread the word about the joys of rhyming poetry.

Rhyme offers a golden opportunity to readers and writers of all ages to improve literacy so I hope my books will inspire them to read and perhaps write their own verses.

Di Castle

LIFE

Should I Wear Floral?

Should I wear floral, the teeny kind,
That will cover my stomach and rolling behind?
Why wear white, which shows each grumpy lump,
And refuses to hide my dowager hump?

Should I wear floral – a long cotton blouse?
That hides what is me, the size of a house!
White on the backside, looming large,
Almost as wide as a waterway barge!

Should I wear floral, is it apt for my age?
Should I give up the white and change it to beige?
I've given up stripes that go left to right,
So perhaps now's the time to give up on white.

Should I wear floral, like all of my friends,
Who cover and hide wobbly tops, sides and ends?
Shall I give up the skimpy and short, now I'm stout,
And large spots that light up the parts that stick out?

Should I wear floral on my bosomy bits,
So it billows on brassieres rather than fits?
Would flowers hide bandy and bow-legged stance
With stalks, twigs and leaves plus various plants?

Should I wear floral, mixed colours and prints
That some put on windows and label it chintz?
Should I pass by the patterns rich, bright and swirling,
And ignore clothes that cling to my curves fast
unfurling?

I've given up shorts and now cover my knees.
I've given up skirts that blow up in the breeze.
For who wants to see flesh so puckered and pocked,
Or set sights on joints that are now firmly locked?

Should I wear floral? I need to know now,
Do plain clothes render me the size of a cow?
Could flowers disguise my increasing girth
And prevent all those youngsters from gurgling mirth?

D. A. Horn.

No… why should I disguise of what I am proud?
I'll wear what I like, plain colours and loud.
I'll show off my cleavage despite all the wrinkles.
Bra straps and g-strings might rouse a few twinkles!

For why should I worry if my dress does offend?
I haven't much time left, I'm nearing my end.
Don't want to wear awful florally frocks.
Wanna look smart when I'm put in my box!

Why I'd Like a New Body

Too much to do, is my plea,
And far too little time.
Each day the mirror tells me
I'm getting past my prime.

Body mousse and mud packs
Are all to no avail.
To get a younger body now
Would take a fairy tale.

It's not the turkey or the pud
That's got me in this mess.
It's kids and men and lack of cash
That's brought on all the stress.

I just can't fit in all the things
I dearly want to do.
It's a faster body that I need
Not one that's just brand new.

I've done the jogs, I've tried the jerks,
Health foods and iron pills.
I've scrapped the fags and stopped the booze
And still can't run up hills.

The quicker that I go, it seems
The slower I become.
Grey hairs, lines and skirts too tight
Defeat this older mum.

So if I win a health farm week
With this silly rhyme
I'll send my other half instead
Because I don't have the time!

Written sometime between 1983 and 1987 in response to a competition in a Sunday newspaper to win a week at a health farm. Needless to say I didn't win.

When I Was A Girl
with apologies to Gilbert and Sullivan

When I was a girl, I served a term
As office girl in an attorney's firm.
I wore high heels and a very short skirt
And made my mark as the office flirt.
That kind of mark so suited me
That soon I was promoted to the top of the tree.

As a shorthand typist my in-tray overflowed.
There were holes in my paper and my shorthand was
quite slow.
The only task I knew how to do
Was put on my make-up in the ladies loo.
That make up did so well for me
That soon I was promoted to the top of the tree.

After a while a girl fell sick
And they needed an assistant who was quick and slick.
So I put on a suit for the interview
With a low-necked blouse which I hoped would woo.
That low-necked blouse did so well for me
That soon I was promoted to the top of the tree.

A few years passed and I was bored
As up the ladder I slowly clawed.
I thought to myself this will never be for me.
I'd rather teach students in a College of FE.
Teaching girls did so well for me
I was sure I'd be promoted to the top of the tree.

But as a teacher I went right down the pan.
I never kept to my lesson plan.
My scheme of work was a terrible farce
And I always seemed to be late for my class.
Being late for class everyone could see
I'd never be promoted to the top of the tree.

But very soon I learnt what it took
To get a promotion in the college book.
I wrote lots of memos about nothing very much
And went to lots of meetings just to keep in touch.
That kind of touch so suited me
That soon I was promoted to the top of the tree.

So young girls all wherever you may be
If you want to rise to the top of the tree.
If your brain's not fettered to a Wang★ or IBM★
Never mind you can still be a right little gem.

Stick close to your desk and very soon you'll be
Given that promotion to the top of the tree.

★Wang and IBM were among the first word processors
we saw in Uxbridge College (previously Uxbridge
Technical College)

A Belated Birthday Wish

Sorry, Jill, forgot the day
To send the birthday card.
Please accept this verse instead
So friendship won't be marred.

No doubt you feel as young as ever
Even though we know
The time when life begins
Is not too long to go.

They say the middle years are best.
You're neither young nor old.
Still young enough to have a fling
And old enough to be more bold.

But others say they think these years
Must be the very worst.
For when you see a dishy man
A young girl gets there first.

Some people your age want a thrill
And join an evening class,
To learn to type or sew or write
Sitting on their… seat.

Take heed from one who's seen them drop
From fatigue and middle-aged spread.
Learning skills, new and nifty
Before they fall down dead.

Remember when Rog is on a trip
He'll meet some girls much younger
And for his body lithe and limber
They're bound to yearn and hunger.

So to keep your man and match the pace
You must lead a healthy life.
Join Keep Fit, aerobics, dancing
Become the perfect wife.

No problem when you flop in chair
Looking such a sight.
You'll say, 'Thank God, the man's away,
I'll get some sleep tonight.'

So birthdays come and birthdays go
I hope you got your present.
The next time that you get it,
Will be in Hoylake Crescent.

The Plastic Friend

*– when personally addressed 0% balance transfer offers flooded
through the letterboxes of the UK*

She had a new year resolute
Not to spend on credit card.
But when you see the sales round here
Not buying is quite hard.

Her other half said cut them up.
Her daughters said the same
But then an offer came in post,
Which clearly had her name.

Six months for nothing – that sounds good!
What a bargain there!
She transferred all the balances
So she didn't have a care.

Seems like it was just yesterday
That offer came through post.
But now six months have gone and passed,
More offers she could boast.

She transferred further balances
The aim to cut the cost,
But somehow all those calculations
Have left her looking lost.

There's now more on those credit cards
And though she pays each time,
The balances are creeping up.
She hasn't got a dime!

Denise A. Horn.

September Daze

– dedicated to all my ex-colleagues in Further Education

A brand new year in Further Ed.
Enrolment joys in store.
Interviewing students
And meetings with furore.

The leader's gone – they know not why.
Rooms locked and desks gone too.
No-one told the teachers
Prep must be done in loo.

Staffrooms moved, staff in a state.
No admin bod in sight.
No time to look, have to teach.
New vetted staff are slight.

Desks left dumped in the gym.
A heap of files to sort.
Where to sit? All chairs have gone!
Tempers now are fraught.

No-one to help, all tied up
Seeing wannabees,
With grades too low for grander place.
'Let me come here, please.'

Few students speak our language
But nothing can be said.
Must go to in-house classes
And learn their tongue instead.

New students with long beards and hair.
Not sure if girls or boys.
Equal ops means mustn't ask
Such puzzles. Oh the joys!

New staffroom sees a battle
For window seat with view,
Of staff cars with their rust and grime
And students' cars brand new!

Humping desks, Jean and Jane
Are side by side again,
Talking health and safety
And retirement with back pain?

Hunt is on for course assignments,
But the writer left last term,
Taking masters with her
To teach at other firm.

Forms to fill, ticking boxes
Takes priority.
Another happy start
September in FE.

The Big Blue Bird
(2001)

Small boy sits in the big blue bird.
His eyes are all agog.
Take off! He gazes out in awe
Through tiny window into fog.

What's this? What's that? Oooooh here we go!
Now the safety talks.
He takes a pull at safety belt
Then up the aisle he walks.

Back in his seat, we start to move
And the bird begins to soar.
Now he's sounding like a lion
Letting out a roar.

Screeching like a fire engine.
A siren at its worst.
Sitting alongside of me.
My ear drums fit to burst.

Now come sweets from those in charge.
They're rattled to and fro.
Cup to cup as arcade coins.
He's shouting, 'Go, go, go!'

19

In shrill loud tone, his voice so loud
Until excitement blew.
Just my luck to get small boy
The first time that he flew!

Why Can't I Go... To That Place?

Why can't I go to uni?
Dons say I'm one of those
Who has much less to offer.
Correct? We'll see. Who knows!

Star performer in my school!
I must be up to scratch.
My A Levels were graded high.
I should be quite a catch.

But other applicants, you said,
Were more suited for a place.
But remember, dons, my grades were gained
By harder work, and faster pace.

Communicator at my side
Ensures equality.
Can't I, as all my hearing peers
Enter university?

For despite my lifelong struggle,
To lipread and to speak,
Discrimination made a call,
With reasons thin and weak.

Denise A. Horn.

Lipreading sometimes lets us down.
People's mouth shapes can be poor.
Try reading lips of hearing folk
Who gesture, shout and roar!

One sense less makes sharper four.
We never miss a sign.
Those with sound have far to go
To match their grades to mine.

22

Here's hoping that another place
Will see my full potential.
Perhaps forget the red brick call
And apply to one provincial?

The inspiration for this poem was the rejection in
August 2002 by a prestigious university of profoundly
deaf Anastasia Fedotova despite her 6 A grade A Levels
in Maths, Further Maths, Physics, Chemistry, Biology
and General Studies. She was later offered places at
two other universities.

2003

Now kiss goodbye to 2002.
The year when rain and floods came through.
Oil and Tony's Iraq spat
And cricket ball not hitting bat.

So while they're looking through the files
To check on oil and Bush's wiles,
We could ponder on the weapons' inspect
Or the spin on truth we might suspect.

We had a tip-top Jubilee.
Brian May on palace roof.
Royal waves and flypasts
While corgis gave a woof.

Three tenths up, the house price ball.
Housing shortage? Not for all!
If we ban asylum seeker
Will this make the market weaker?

MP likes curry but is not wise.
Another MP in prison now lies
For bedding girls and causing scandal.
Perhaps write a book, then freedom wrangle?

Will Gordon Brown balance the books?
And pay attention to his looks?
What has happened to our gold?
His budget more a stranglehold.

Will Tony send our lads to war?
Or walk the talk with more jaw jaw?
Jetting around the warming globe
Seeking some celestial robe.

Paedophiles will all be freed.
Tone will legalise the weed.
And when he catches Osama bin Laden
Bet your life he'll get a pardon.

Global warming leaves us chilly
And Back to Basics now looks silly.
Schoolings out, teachers weary,
Computer screens and eyes so bleary.

Friends on holiday in Croatia
Feel safer there than far off Asia.
So welcome in the brand new year
2003 – nothing to fear?

Mum Of The Year Award

Mum of the Year? I doubt it's mine
Although grown kids are well and fine.
They've flown the nest but I don't pine.
I'm never one to toe the line.

Housework left for evening time.
Cannot miss the sunshine prime.
Clocks all different, constant chime.
Late for school? Tis not a crime.

Ballet classes, many shows.
Costumes made, but missed the bows.
One side higher than the other.
Who made yours? Not your mother!

Dresses to match for wedding day.
Till later when they're out to play.
Stitches are loose, seams are parting.
Expert says, 'Should put a dart in?'

Hems fell down, necklines drooped.
Could see your tummy when you stooped.
Soon gave up that sewing lark.
Was not the way I'd make my mark?

Cooking wasn't any better.
Much preferred to write a letter.
Food was burnt or stuck to pan.
Could never find the heart of man!

Christmas pudding in plastic pot
Melted from the steam, too hot.
Brandy sauce too strong for kids.
Bread sauce lumpy, stuck to lids.

And when it came to homework drudge
My rusty skills I had to fudge.
Then your friend had a higher grade
So put my effort in the shade.

It seems I won't get TV fame
Hearing someone call my name.
Another mother has won the prize
For Mum of the Year. No surprise!

New Shoes

New shoes, lovely shoes?
Expensive shoes for towns?
Warm shoes, cosy boots?
For walking on the Downs?

Denise A. Horn.

Tight shoes, loose shoes?
Send them to the dumps.
New brogues or welly boots?
Ballet shoes or pumps?

High heels, sling backs?
Cuban heels or flat?
Pretty ones with glitter studs?
For weddings with a hat?

Shoes with buckles, shoes with laces,
Plimsolls, trainer brands.
Open sandals, flip flops, crocs
For walking on the sands.

Red shoes, blue shoes?
White shoes, to match?
Assistant running everywhere,
To find another batch!

What's in a Thumb?

*January 2002 when we still had
to sign for credit card payments*

Oh RSI, I'm hurting some.
You've travelled far into my thumb.
It's swollen large, red and numb.
RSI makes life so glum.

We never credit digit thumb
Until it's acting rather dumb.
Getting in the way of all.
Pain threshold is off the wall.

How did I get this RSI?
The question is, not how? but why?
Was it throwing 'ballie' for my dog
Or dragging her from local bog?

Was it painting fence for hours and hours?
Or planting out my new spring flowers?
Perhaps the culprit is this typing
I doubt it's cleaning, or window wiping?

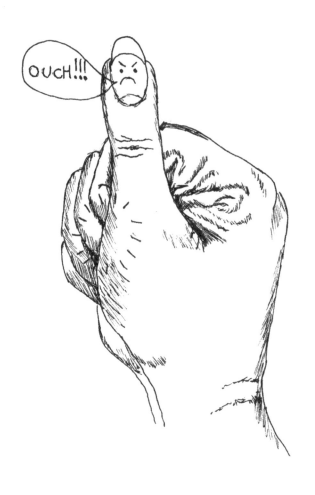

Denise A. Horn

Now I can't work this drat computer
Or give a toot on scooter hooter.
Can't open can or jar lid turn.
Hungry husband looks quite stern.

Shopping's out – can't carry bags.
Can only wear loose fitting rags.
Can't fasten buttons or pull up zips.
Can't tie up laces or paint my lips.

No credit card, can't sign my name,
And when cheques bounce my thumb I'll blame.
Can't hold a pen to write a letter.
When will this RSI get better?

But wait! There's much I still can do.
So when I get on phone to you.
Beware! I have no jobs which beckon
And nought on TV is what I reckon.

So one less digit leaves me free.
Natter, chatter, gossip. Yippee!
Nothing wrong with voice of course.
I'll talk and talk until I'm hoarse!

Fat Chances

2002

English children, getting fat.
Computer, TV, Sofa Brat.
Not their fault that they're not slim.
Blame the Government, especially 'him'!

No PE, the school gym's taken
For AS resits and admin makin'.
Sports fields sold, no place to run
And not p.c. to say you've won.

No healthy food, the dinner's junk.
Enter slow the 10 stone hunk.
No skipping ropes or balls in view.
Playground games are now taboo.

Ferried to school in mother's car.
School's in next road but, 'tis too far!
Help! Every room must have a telly.
Door-to-door lifts leave legs of jelly.

Bussed to pool ten miles away.
No time to swim – traffic delay.
Never mind missing an hour of dance.
League tables don't value pins and prance.

At home can't play, their bikes are stowed.
Freed offender lives down the road.
Litter in parks so cannot race
And too much traffic outside their place.

Homework these days must be done
Sitting bribed with sticky bun.
Hours on a computer gets a good mark.
Walk to the library? No, too dark!

Teachers teaching lists of facts.
Not real life but Blair's diktats.
Mum's out working to pay tuition,
Technician, optician and dietician!

Happy Holidays
2002

Airport parking is a bind.
First the car park you must find.
Then get the luggage out the boot.
Oops! Spilt a drink on travel suit!

Buses come three times an hour.
Crowds of travellers feeling sour.
Cannot all get on the bus.
Partner grumpy! Makes a fuss.

Why three pieces? Rucksack too!
What shall we with the carriers do?
Need to change, no free loo!
August booking, now I rue.

Pick a trolley, stand and wait.
Broken wheel! Found too late!
So we lug the cases via
Moving stairs to queue up higher.

Then the treadmill – walk along
Midst the teeming holi throng.
Shane and Trace have all the gear.
Rucksacks bumping in my rear.

Now at check-in have we got
All the things that we should not?
One look at partner, then the fears.
Has he brought the toenail shears?

At last we've checked in, can relax.
But partner wants to send a fax!
Or post a letter! Oh what next?
Must teach him how to send a text!

Sit in lounge and take in turns
To shop and spend more than he earns.
Need the toilet! 'Too late!' he roared
Numbered gate is up on board!

Struggle on more rubber motion.
Have I got the right sun lotion?
But didn't get gate number right.
Partner eyes are not too bright.

Now I fight my way to seat.
Oh, this next part is hard to beat!
Obese lady does overflow
Half my seat hidden below!

Now that's better. Here's the trolley.
Just need lots of foreign lolly.
Two drinks up, I'm in the mood.
Hurry up and bring the food.

Feeling happy now I know
Why I'm going where I go.
Who cares if neighbour shouts and swears.
It's holiday! Forget your cares!

Doris In The Choir

Doris liked to sing a lot.
She joined a choir to stop the rot.
She sang each Thursday and what's more.
She practised daily behind bathroom door.

She thought it would be such a doddle,
But at end of term she had to waddle
On to the stage to sing in choir
In front of villagers and Squire.

She had to wear a special dress
And make her hair look less a mess.
She also needed hearing aid
To time crescendo and then her fade.

But on the stage her earpiece dropped
And to her dismay all singing stopped.
In back row she missed her cues.
Large soprano blocked her views.

So Conductor put her in the front
But Lil behind her gave a shunt.
Twas not Lil's fault but zimmer frame
Which for this accident was to blame.

As Doris fell on string musician
Her skirt around her neck gave vision.
The fiddler did continue playing
While Doris upside down was swaying.

With only fiddler's bow in view,
Doris missed her solo cue.
Lil was quick to steal her thunder.
Sang out for loud applause to plunder.

Eventually Doris came right side up,
But those choir mates had given up.
An empty room – they'd all gone home O.
And left her on her own alone O.

We Shall Remember Them

Thank you, divorcing couple,
For selling me your house.
Thank you, older neighbours,
Who live as quiet mouse.

Thank you, dear inventor,
For easing daily chores.
Thank you, bright green plastic friend,
For spotless vacuumed floors.

Thank you, girl in wheelchair,
For reminding me I'm healthy.
Thank you, the beggar who lies in the street,
For reminding me I'm wealthy.

Thank you to those who invented the wheel,
For pram and bike and car.
Thank you those who forged travel by air,
Now we holiday wide and far.

Thanks go to all of the suffragettes,
Who fought to give women the vote,
And thank you, computer, for helping me now,
To put words on the page for this note.

Mad or what?

(2005 – a new social trend is 'skiing' or
spending the kids' inheritance)

My offspring say I am quite mad.
They do despair of me.
I know they talk behind my back,
Say I'm getting out my tree.

I see them eye each other,
When I re-iterate my dreams.
They roll their eyes and wink a lot
Distract me with ice creams.

I tell them I've been shopping.
I hear them ooh and sigh.
I can't remember what I've bought
Or where I've been or why.

They tell me that quite soon
They'll put me in a home
And take away my internet
Where I surf the web and roam.

They'll take away my credit cards
My cheque book and my pin.
Put warnings out in charity shops
So they don't let me in.

But getting old is not so bad.
It has so many plusses.
Like free eye tests and fuel allowance.
And passes for the buses.

So I'll keep searching websites
For the route to youth, the gist.
I'll keep sending silly poems,
Get their knickers in a twist.

But while I have a stair lift
I can still live out my dreams.
I can still send silly poems
And links to hair-brained schemes.

I'll get a mobile scooter
By searching on the web.
I'll imagine I am famous
A really great celeb!

I know they worry when they see
Their inheritance balance waning,
But I'll keep spending all my cash
So my bank account keeps draining.

It's Just My Age
2005

Now I'm sixty, perhaps I'll be
Arthritic in my hip and knee.
Maybe it's time for headscarf and rollers.
Have crowns and plates instead of molars?

Shall I sit in rocking chair?
Knit woolly socks for Oldies Fair?
Stay at home, nice cup of tea?
Watch Rich and Judy on TV?

Now I have my Senior Passes
I scowl at schoolboys through my glasses.
I'll buy myself a walking stick
To get to Bingo double quick!

I hear that flannelette's the rage
For someone getting to my age.
But, do I care if now I lose it
So much bother when I use it.

Well, no I don't, I won't and can't.
Old and grey, well that I aren't.
I'll rock and roll and rave and shout,
Be never in and always out!

48

I'll join the over-sixties club
If they meet in local pub.
I'll wear the clothes that 'aren't quite right',
Gawdy, skimpy and far too bright!

I'll dye my hair the latest shade,
Orange with a hint of jade.
And now my grammar and memory's gone,
I think I'll stop this carry on!

49

Limericks

There was once a happy old Snapper.
With his camera he looked quite a dapper.
He won lots of prizes
And cups of all sizes
While his photos caused much of a flapper.

*****

There was a young man called Barry,
Who thought he was happy as Larry.
Then he met JKR
Who said they'd go far
With a character we now know as Harry.

*****

A computer whizzkid known as Danny,
Was internet fit, wise and canny.
But emails went astray,
When he went away,
To sort out his client called Granny.

*****

There once was a man who liked yoga
Who dressed in a short Roman toga.
He posed for his new published book
And the crowds all hurried to look
Until a policeman arrested the ogre!

★★★★★

There once was a young man called Ryan
Whose stories could often be trying
But he kept up the patter
Just like the Mad Hatter
And ignored all the moaning and sighing.

★★★★★

Denise A. Horn.

Retirement

What's for lunch?
He always asks.
What are you doing?
Daily tasks!

Where's the salt?
On the table.
What are you doing?
All I am able!

What's for dinner?
My answer is rude.
Where are you going?
Shopping for food!

What will you get?
Some milk and some bread.
When will you be back
So I can be fed?

Did you buy cake?
Oh why does he nag?
You've forgotten my paper!
My shoulders now sag.

Why are you crying?
Why look so sad…?

…I'm remembering workdays
And the peace that I had.

Smoking Fad
ode to giving up smoking 2001

I've given up the smoking fad
As my lungs were full of ash.
No longer do I know the price
Or even have the cash.

I puffed when twenties were a pound.
Then slowly up they soared
Until I paid a fiver
I could barely ill afford.

The reason for my abstinence
Is easy to explain.
I joined a choir but only squeaked
The breathing was a pain.

I couldn't take a gasp
When my voice cried out for air.
It spoilt the choir's rendition
And brought director's glare.

So I threw away the packet
The ashtrays and the stubs.
So I could have my hands free
When drinking in the pubs.

But now I hate the smell of fags
My nose curls, wrinkles too.
The whiff, tobacco trace on clothes
From smokers sitting next to you.

Ex-smokers whine more than those
Who never touched the weed.
They smell a smoker from a mile
And run away at speed.

They wonder why you change your seat
But like the man of drink
No-one likes a smoker
With clothes and hair that stink.

So smokers please give up your sin.
Spare a thought for us.
Spend your money on gin instead
Then we won't make a fuss.

SWANAGE

– a selection of poems
celebrating this wonderful area
of Dorset

Swanage

I remember, I remember,
The day we found this town.
We travelled in from Studland,
Through Ulwell and then down.

The vision, one hot evening
With children laughing, playing.
Sandcastles, litter in the bins,
Boats with sails a swaying.

No place to park, we could not stop
But, as promised, we returned,
Later in the summer
For a weekend break we'd earned.

And on return, late summer
A similar moving sight.
We walked our collie on the Down
At dusk in magic light.

We gazed down over fairyland
Breathless, awed, inspired.
We stood, we watched and knew we'd found
What our hearts had long desired.

April Day

I walked up Down on April Day
And gazed out down on Swanage Bay.
The hawthorn whispered silver sounds.
Its blossom sight all soon astounds.

The horses ran up Durlston cliffs.
White backs breaking shipwrecked skiffs.
The spray spreads sprawling in the wind.
On to the rocks the water's pinned.

The pier beneath, its arm outstretched
Welcomes all with cameras fetched.
A copse within the Down lies hidden
From which dogs come when they are bidden.

Sea mist has now become fast thinned
As wind makes waves turn and rescind.
Now Isle of Wight rears up her head.
Says, 'Don't look there, look here instead!'

8 April 2002

Summer Road Hog

Get a move on
Sluggish lout.
Car so slow
On your day out.

Look at this!
Look at that!
Slowing down
In your funny hat.

But we must work
Us local peeps.
For roof above our head
For keeps.

So dawdle, linger
Drink the view.
Like no-one's on this road
But you.

Where are we now?
At window – rage!
No right change
For ferry stage.

See the boats!
There's the sea!
What's that leaving
From the quay?

Children hanging
Inside out and upside down
about to rampage
through our town.

But we don't mind the grockels
Wandering through the town
We need our summer visitors
Before the sun goes down.

Oh, to be in Swanage

Oh to be in Swanage
Now that Winter's here.
The noise of tourists fast abates
Until they fix next year's dates.

When car park's full and beach is packed
Our parking space has been hijacked.
Now we can park our own four wheels.
Shop shelves now have special deals.

No more litter to pick up.
Empty carton, plastic cup.
No more bags beside the bin
Because they cannot get it in.

Now we walk the empty street.
Enjoy the Indian summer heat.
Take the bus and get a seat.
Autumn in Swanage is hard to beat.

Studland beaches now so clear.
Winter walks are lovely here.
Coastal path and Swanage Down
And then a coffee in the town.

Moon

I walked down to the seafront.
I saw a wonderous sight.
The moon was shining on the bay.
The sea was fiery bright.

The glimmer and the shimmer
Snatched my breath away.
I stood and gazed on God's good work.
This light upon the bay.

Yes, full moon shines on Swanage Bay.
A silver circle gleams.
The people here are truly blessed
By heaven's earthward beams.

It costs not even a penny
To gaze upon this sight.
A view of Nature smiling
On this bleak mid winter's night.

There can be nothing better.
This gift of Nature's craft.
God's love is glowing, radiant.
A shining, silver shaft.

Tourists do not see it.
Unseen in summer light.
We only see horizon lit
On cold dark winter's night.

The tourists have their summer.
They flock here every day
But I prefer still winter
And this glorious moonlit bay.

Best Bliss

There can be no bliss.
It defies every time
As the new born scent
To a mum in her prime.

New babies are special
But there's nothing so good…
Not even your favourites –
The pubs, drinks and food.

No food, even French
Can supply what's decreed.
Siesta on bench
Are we all agreed?

No matter how pretty
How exquisite the view.
There's nothing can beat
What I'm telling you.

Don't think that I'm telling
Fake truth through my teeth.
What I say is the best
Is not sun on a heath.

Nor sunshine, nor tan.
Nor those holiday trips.
Nor girls with their jeans
Swimming down off their hips.

No! It's in winter the beach
Deserted and bare.
Sea lashing, wind rushing
With nobody there!

And summer at low tide.
Walking barefoot on sand.
This ultimate bliss.
This seaside so grand!

October

Friday night
Streets jammed
Car park full
One trolley
Wonky wheel
Swarming mob
Hiking boots

Ouch! Little toe
No bread
No veg
No oven chips
No fishfingers
No baked beans
Leaking milk
Cracked eggs
Squashed cake!

Six trolleys
Piled high
Junk food
Wine and beer
One checkout
Faulty scanner
Long queue
Tea Break…

Noisy kids
Crying baby
Screaming toddler
Bicker, bicker
Row, row
Red faces
White faces
Half-term!

MORE LIFE

They're Always There

They're always there,
Tattooed men and yobs so loud.
The iphones, and the ding ding ring.
The scruffy looking crowd.

They're always there on rush hour trains,
The teens, the mobile addict pains.
Gurgly coughs and throaty laughs.
Stomach burps not done in halves.

They're always there, with noisy kids,
People who click, click coffee cup lids.
And slurp and burp, blow bubbles through straws,
Chew and crunch apples in their jaws.

They're always there, the kids on our bus,
With noses oozing streams of pus.
One is wailing, 'want a wee!'
Too late, it's dribbling… right near me!

They're always there, at the beach near us
With children who scream and make lots of fuss.
Then dig dry sand and let it fly
Floating upwards into your eye.

They're always there, too close on the beach
With parents shouting within our reach.
They pitch their tent, then start to smoke.
Ignore us when we cough and choke.

When wet they shelter in our doors
Let dogs jump up with dirty paws.
Dripping cagoules and stinky shoes
Black bag ready for puppy's poos.

They always park up tight alongside
Whenever we drive to park and ride.
Despite the vacant fifty spaces
They've passed with blank and blinkered faces.

They're always there in the waiting room,
The know-it-all and speakers of doom.
Mindless, endless, brainless chatter
Airing views on senseless matter.

They're always there with big loud voices
Discussing at length their pub food choices.
The winner is a yawning bore.
Whatever you've got, he's got more!

They're always there, in the restaurant,
Laughing and shouting for what they want.
They're always there, at parents' night
Telling all their kids are bright.

They're always there in the shopping queue
Their trolley gently nudging you.
Terminal refuses the card ahead.
As they try three more, you wish them dead!

Family Christmas

Christmas, birthdays, celebration treats!
Funerals, Weddings, family meets!

Mum is stressed about the food.
Dad is in a grumpy mood.

Grandma didn't want to come.
Dad didn't want his in-law mum.

Then a row between the brothers
On who got what from departed others.

Baby sicks up on fluffy rug.
Grandma laughs and drops beer mug.

Dad shouts, 'You won't come again!'
Grandma cheers, laughs like a drain.

Rants, 'Rue the day you met my daughter!'
Dad calls police just to thwart her.

Police take Grandma to a cell
But refuse to take the kids as well.

Now Mum and Dad do row a lot
About Gran's bail and who pays what!

Dad says, 'She aint worth a penny,'
And Mum, at Christmas, hasn't any.

So Grandma stays in cell for the season!
Laughs to herself for real good reason.

No more celebration 'do'!
Queueing as uncle's drunk in loo.

No looking daft as deaf aid's broken
And cannot hear the words they've spoken.

No more sitting in the corner
With foot in mouth as no-one warned her.

And never's better than being late
With daughter's good-for-nothing mate!

Next year before that celebration
Someone please plan arbitration.

Sopranos

(with apologies to Gilbert and Sulllivan)

Never say 'I am only in the chorus' as without a chorus there is no show.

We are the very model of the Operatic chorus sops.
Who put on great performances, that buzz… until the curtain drops.
We take all our instructions with a duty so reliable.
We need to get it right so all reviews are good and viable.

Our leader is so cheerful that she keeps us feeling up, you know.
We Operatic chorus sops preparing for our brand new show.
Our leader gets us going and she really is incredible
Withstanding interferences from some you might call 'meddle bull'.

Withstanding interferences from some you might call 'meddle bull'

The pianist is playing hard and covering up mistakes, you know,

And costume lady's running round with measure tape and things to sew.
Treasurer is selling tickets, sorting stats to fill each row
We're Operatic chorus sops preparing for our brand new show.

We're very good at singing when we have the words in front of us
But leader says to face the front and leave the sheet away from us.

84

She says we sing it once or twice and then we're told again to go
We hope this all gets sorted before April when the show's in flow

We hope that this gets sorted before April when the show's in flow.

We don't think we are ready for a show that soon will go on stage.
We are still learning words, crescendos, breathing and… must hold the page.
And now we're told to move around, our brains go into overload,
We cannot do it all without us going into overload.

We cannot do it all without us going into overload.

We have to make a hat that now is looking very complicate,
For singing Ascot whatsit and we mustn't walk on much too late.
Yes, singing Ascot whatsit is what really makes our brains go pops,
We mustn't come on late or find ourselves on stage without our props.

In short we mustn't come on late or find ourselves without our props.

We are the very model of the Operatic chorus sops.
Put at the back if we're too fat and old and grey in case we flop.
We miss our cues, forget our words and cannot dance like dainty birds
And now conductor splits us up into three groups he calls three thirds.

Conductor splits us up into three thirds to make us learn our words.

We are the very model of the Operatic chorus sops
Who keep the show a buzzing on the stage until the curtain drops.
We've learnt our words, we know our thirds but now it is finale time
Our brains go pop, the words now stop but never mind we'll use some mime.

Yes, we still keep the show a buzzing on the stage til curtain drops.
'Cos we're the very model of the Operatic chorus sops!

The Octogenarian

Let's give a cheer for Grandad R
Now propping up the local bar.
He's got to eighty, what a feat!
It's why we're here on Oldie Street.

Octogenarian at last
Expounding knowledge of engines vast,
And mowers which he tends and tinkers,
While wearing masks and safety blinkers.

Now tractors do have parts quite fickle
Oozing oil into a trickle.
But such is Grandad's expertise
Boss only has to utter 'please?'.

And Grandad's off to look and see.
Where it needs some TLC.
Is it a canoe or pedalo?
Just hang in there, Grandad will know.

Denise A. Horn.

Shopping

People shopping unawares
New goods won't take away their cares.
'Must have now' the modern state.
No such thing as save and wait.

Wardrobe bulging, doors won't shut.
Full of last week's arcade glut.
Don't they know we wear not much
Of what is hidden, out of touch?

Off to sales their brains are fizzing.
Madness – credit cards are whizzing.
Black Friday brings the great stampede.
Tug of war with TV lead.

Online buys, one click it takes.
Designer label, not the fakes.
Parcels piled outside the door,
On the table, on the floor.

Downloads, emails, sales in flow.
Put in your password, here we go.
Something for him, something for me.
Add some more for postage free.

Cheapie supermarket trips.
Trolleys packed with frozen chips.
Now can't shut the freezer door.
To solve the problem, just eat more.

High Street full of charity shops.
Rails of dresses, skirts and tops,
Bought on a whim, now thrown out.
New gear, each year. 'Want, want,' they shout!

Bookshops dying as we browse.
Blame greedy giants and cash cows.
Gone the throbbing, heaving mob.
Online shop has done the job.

Imports cheap but watch them crease.
They're buying clothes two pounds apiece.
Nice look but doubt they'll last a season.
So back to shopping with good reason.

Shopping crazy, shopping spree!
The myth that buying makes them free.
Alerts on phone, hear the bell
Trapped in their manic shopping hell.

Complainers

Some people always have to moan.
The weather's bad, the tv's trash.
Cardboard meals, tasteless muck.
Half-cooked veg and lumpy mash.

The council never does its job.
There's litter in the parks.
The roads are full of potholes.
And those planners please the sharks.

The local operatic tickets
Are far too high they say.
There'll soon be cuts to moan about
With a freeze on public pay.

The trains are running late, oh dear!
The leaves are on the line.
Trees fallen down and blocking tracks.
'Do something!' they all whine.

The swimming pool is far too cold
The sauna is too hot.
Those forever wanting
What they haven't got.

Denise A. Horn.

Too much rain, now a drought.
The gardens need the rains.
Local transport workers strike
So now there are no trains.

'They' should do this, 'They' should do that
But who are 'them' and 'they'?
The moaners had their chance last year.
Where were 'they' on polling day?

No, you shouldn't be complaining.
You should be feeling blessed.
For if you do have children.
You know life is the best.

And if you have no children
Your life is far less stressed.
You suit yourself and live your life,
With a home that's far less messed.

So stop this constant moaning.
Facebook, Twitter, strife.
Start counting all your blessings
Enjoy your chance in life.

What Happened to the Answerphone

What happened to the answerphone
With its bright red winking light,
Beeping with a message
When you'd been out at night?

What happened to the answer phone
Awaiting your return?
A message says, 'I love you.
For you I ever yearn.'

What happened to the answer phone
Poor Grandma doesn't get it.
She says, 'Hello,' and then once more.
'You must be out. Forget it!'

This time a message, not so good.
The bank has left its mark.
'Please come to see the manager,
To discuss your shopping lark.'

The most important message
You find is incomplete.
The answerphone now is full.
All you hear is 'Pete'.

Denise A. Horn.

Pete could be the plumber
Or the man you met last night?
Not sure if you can work it out
When your mornings aren't too bright.

And then there is the breathing
Heavy, panting, low.
Just to make you nervous
And wonder where to go.

But then you hear a squeaky voice
Piping up to give her news.
'Nanny, I've just had a fall
And got a great big bruise.'

Excuse Me If I Smash Your Phone

Excuse me if I smash your phone,
And dump it down the drain.
We really do not want to hear,
'Hello, I'm on the train.'

Excuse me if I smash your phone,
I know you're on this train.
And I'm really not that interested,
In your week-long trip to Spain.

Excuse me if I smash your phone,
The Quiet Zone should do it.
I'd like to splice it from your ear,
And let my shredder chew it.

Excuse me if I smash your phone,
Your ailments make me sick.
You'd better hide it in your bag,
Or I'll grab it double quick.

Excuse me if I smash your phone,
Your eyes don't leave the screen.
We're on a date, our eyes should meet,
Are mine blue, or brown or green?

Excuse me if I smash your phone,
And dump it in the bin.
Its silly jingle woke me up,
And made an awful din.

Excuse me if I smash your phone,
But this is better, honey.
I'll take it, dial overseas,
And cost you lots of money.

Excuse me if I smash your phone,
They should legislate against them.
Make a law, impose some fines,
But for now I'll gladly smash 'em!

Look Down Generation – 2015

The Look Down Generation
Ignores the clear blue sky.
They look down, look down, look down,
As life is passing by.

The Look Down Generation
Logged in and in the Cloud.
Sh, sh, I've got the Wifi.
Just wait. Don't speak so loud.

The Look Down Generation's here.
Mum, one-handed, in the road.
Her precious pramload heading
For a lorry's dangerous load.

Look Down Generation scowls.
They've forgotten how to smile.
They've forgotten how to talk.
They look down all the while.

Written English out of date.
Shorter, shorter r 2 b.
The only words the look-downs know
Won't win a spelling bee.

Look down, look down, look down,
On Kindle, app or phone.
Look down, look down, look down,
In a world you've made your own.

Look down, look down, look down,
Reading from a text.
Social skills have gone awry,
Leaving all quite vexed.

Laptop, iPad, mobile too,
Facebook, email, twitter.
Thumbing, reading, flicking, laughing.
Can't relax, they're all a jitter.

Tapping, texting, tagging, timeline,
Adding pictures pressing send.
YouTube, blogs, loads of links.
The world is going round the bend.

The Look Down Generation -
Their baby's looking sad.
They'd rather read a Facebook post
Than chat and make her glad.

The mums don't talk to babies.
They're simply looking down.
Joy now comes from smileys
And Facebook shares in town.

Girl looks down, won't speak to me.
Looking cross, thoughts interrupted.
No time, when asked the way,
Her phone time now disrupted.

Then, jingle, jingle, answer now.
Face time with redundant ear,
Talking loudly, fast and fiery
Flirty talk that all can hear.

Free hand wiggles on the screen.
Not a word to child.
Snapchat, Instagram and Linked.
A lonely world gone wild.

Cruising Crowd

Large liner lies bereft in bay.
While cruisers have gone out.
They ask directions. 'We're from that ship!'
'How to get there?' They point and shout.

In the town with pavements packed.
Shops are heaving, there's nowhere free
From laden wallets, noisy show-offs.
Buying tat and that; on a spree.

While musing round the tiny shops
We must avoid the cruising mobs.
Marching, mooting, munching
Every street vibrates and throbs.

In special places, hushed and praying
Cruisers shout with raucous voices.
And in cathedrals, churches, we see
A sheepish line of tour guide choices.

The leader holds a flag aloft
The cruisers walk like sheep,
Blocking every pavement
As they plod along six deep.

Haggling, bargaining, banter, talking.
Chest puffed out for strutting not walking.
Milling, marauding, mouthing loud,
Cranky, creaking, cruisy crowd

Guest Poem on New Words in 2015

By Helen MacDonald

With gritted teeth and raised BP I've learned to compromise
When hearing words like DIGIVERSE, CHILLAX and DIARISE,
And not directly have a fit when listening to the news.
Our language changes all the time and some it may amuse!

My moisturiser's not just smooth, it soothes and MATTIFIES
For it's a COSMACEUTICAL, the label states – whatever that implies.
Men aren't just mates, or drinking pals, but now they must have labels.
As having a BROMANCE, by trendy types, like imaginary fables!
But worse maybe is a FRENEMY with which they could contend
For that's a secret rival, who is pretending he's a friend.

And as though we need more labels there's the DEMITARIAN
Who eats a little bit of meat but is mainly vegetarian!

I've also learned a new disease – AFFLUENZA it is named,
Caught by bankers and their like, who claim they can't be blamed
For earning obscene money and spending like a drain
Which causes them anxiety and intensely nervous strain.
It would make it even worse if chased by VIDEORAZZI
Who are video operating types of old-fashioned paparazzi!

And they feed the appetites of star-crazed groups of
FANDOMS
Who stalk their admired target literally in tandem.

I can't leave out the lazy words, coined by the younger
speaker
Who put two words together to make them short and
sleeker.
LATERS and AMAZEBALLS are self-explanatory
But MAGHAGs may be less so, and also defamatory,
For it refers to female editors of US magazines,
Who encourage all the FANDOMS and publish all the
FANZINES!
Worst of all, and finally, there are words akin to slush
If I actually had to say one I would unquestionably blush,
ADORBS, UNFRIEND, EMOJI are words I cannot
stick
In fact, you know, I'd not just blush, I'd be physically sick!

LOVE

Remember?

I remember, I remember,
My Dad when I was small.
Sitting in school audience,
Distinguished, handsome, tall.

Digging in the garden,
Building rockery.
Growing scented flowers,
That my mother loved to see.

Building me a swing,
Toy theatre, dolls house, cot.
What my heart was ever set on,
You could be sure I got.

Through his teeth a unique whistle
Told us exactly where he stood
In a crowd, or off exploring
Beach, common, forest, wood.

Then when my mother passed away,
On pedestal he placed me.
For years he treated and he spoiled
His kindness, goodness graced me.

He was never to be old,
Or needy like some,
Or dependent on homecare
Waiting for carers to come.

He died far too young.
Nicotine took the blame.
But it stopped me from smoking,
And life was never the same.

Life Friend

Love erupted, flashed in a day,
Changed life from slow to fast.
A feisty 'stop 'n go' affair
Which no-one thought would last!

Passion enflamed, excitement aroused,
Sparks kindled electrical charge.
Lack of sleep, jumbled thoughts.
Am I dreaming, is this a mirage?

Treasured are all the laughs you evoke.
The giggles, the touch of the hand.
The secret codes, the wink that declares
Against the world we stand.

Cherishing moments, sharing the chores.
Comfort when news is the worst.
Planning to make special each day.
Thinking and putting each first.

But Love can also show some vexation
When harassed or harassing too.
When lovers forget the meaning of life
And lack compromise of view.

Creative spirits on divergent paths
Separate ways when freedom is favoured.
Brief intermission – rest, and return,
As love and loyalty never wavered.

Precious and valued, you're always there
When others go hurtling by.
Helping me weather the storms of life
And never saying that goodbye.

New Beginnings

What's your name? What do you do?
Opening lines with someone new.
On her own is far from dull
But bonding in haste leaves time to mull!

Last night with many new people she danced
But one stands out – she was entranced.
Will they gel? This is the test.
Will he be like others or not like the rest?

She gave him her number and hopes he will phone.
Fun isn't fun when you're always alone.
She hopes her smile made his heart sing.
But perhaps to him she meant not a thing.

If the phone doesn't ring, oh, should she call him?
Or was the light in the dance hall too dim?
Did she miss the signs that he's married or gay?
Did she give away too much? What did she say?

Did she sound too happy with life as it is?
Being single, not married, not Mrs but Ms?
Did she sound rather cynical, blasé or curt?
Did her manner remind him of times he's been hurt?

Morning time text, then they talk for an hour.
She feels drawn and loses her resolute power.
What will she say, if he asks for a date?
Should she make a move for fear it's too late?

And so it is they arrange to meet.
She'll dress up and go to large pub on main street.
He's fair dressed and, must say, not bad at first look.
And there is one good sign. He holds newspaper and book.

She looks at the paper, not her choice, her spine shivers.
What is she doing? Her legs start the quivers.
He looks up – he's wondering – is this…? Hope it is!
She stares straight ahead. She'll never be his!

Di's Wedding Verse 1988

With apologies to the Bard of Stratford upon Avon
and thanks to Cole Porter for his inspiration via Kiss
Me Kate

To wed or not to wed, that was the question
And A Winter's Tale it became.
So I said, well all right As You Like It
And made Anthony and Cleo seem tame!

He said life with me was a Tempest.
It was worse than Taming the Shrew!
I said give me your Measure for Measure,
Or of nothing there'll be much ado.

He said it's A Midsummer Night's Dream,
But he always was late for a date.
And if music be the food of love,
No wonder I don't put on weight.

He said I'm your Merchant of Venice.
You'll never see Love's Labours Lost.
But then if it's only each Twelfth Night,
More lights through my window could be tossed.

Denise A. Horn.

So if on the Express D'Orient,
I don't meet two gents from Verona,
And I don't become A Merry Wife of Windsor,
I'll remain Bryan's Desdemona!

So to sum up my life with the groom,
A Comedy of Errors I could tell.
We may be no Romeo and Juliet
But remember – All's Well That Ends Well!

Polly

My faithful friend was ageing,
So I thought she'd like a friend
For comfort and companionship
As she slowed down for life's end.

I went inside the compound.
Wire fences all around.
I walked by cages, read the cards
But didn't feel heart pound.

And then behind a large black lad
I spied my heart's desire,
And as I faced this beauty
She lit my heart with fire.

Months passed, we bonded, three of us
With love fast interweaving.
But my heart ached, because I knew
She and I would soon be grieving.

A year went by, the old 'un died.
The young one was demented.
Ran, sniffing, searching, seeking
The friend she so lamented.

Denise M. Horn.

But soon we were a double act,
With cuddles, walks and training.
Adoration in her eyes
Our sadness now fast waning.

And then returned a former love.
Revived our passion flurried.
He fussed her much and plenty
With country walks, less hurried.

Now my ex has dined and stayed,
Our love is well restored.
But now my hound won't look at me,
It's *he* who is adored!

Family Wedding

As there was no best man to tell ribald jokes enough to curl their toes, I decided to provide a substitute.

Our story starts in '63
When two young things had a spree
And in the June of '64
Our groom did enter with a roar.

Years later in Pompei our groom met
A friend of girl whose room he let.
The rest we know without a guess.
Romance blossomed with our Tess.

Groom and bride frolicked on.
Built patio to sit upon.
Good at drives and building ponds
Not to mention all that… gardening.

We all know what you get from that!
A tummy that grows rather fat!
First they had our little Amy
Then along came brother Jamie.

Last winter dates did run amok
Played hide and seek with our groom's... sock.
Now they know that's what you get
From boring Sundays when weather's wet.

News is that we will have some more
Pitter patter on the floor.
Suggest you go to see the Doc
Before I end up in more hock.

So now you're married, T and N,
No more talk of 'Shall we, then?'
Both hoping for a brand new life?
Forget it, folks, you're man and wife!

Denise A. Horn.

LEAVING

Royal Memories
August 1997

Seems yesterday that August night
Our English Rose lost her light.
A royal mother lost in France.
An accident or… perhaps just chance?

Two men still wonder 'Why take her'?
As papers, radio, tv infer.
Driven to death, last fast chase.
Media rueing loss of face.

Kensington Gardens, the flowers adorned
Laid by those who came and mourned.
In disbelief they stood and gazed
Deep in thought, time erased.

Two friends to London on a train.
September light and passing refrain.
Reflecting on the news forlorn
Sad grey Sunday, death at dawn.

Before us the Palace, its presence frigid,
She tried; her brief light easing the rigid.
Flowers strewn, notes lit with kisses.
Our light snuffed out, so much she misses.

Then gun carriage for her bed.
Father, sons and husband led.
Westminster Abbey – a brother's pain.
A light we shall not see again.

Sad royal life ended young.
Lumps in throats when hymns are sung.
Tears from thousands flocking to see
A pageant of our royalty.

Lining route – a silent crowd.
Flowers are thrown and heads are bowed.
No more light on lovely face.
Althorp's lake her resting place.

Easter Day 2002

The Queen Mum's dead
The Queen Mum's dead
Despite intensive coverage
It won't stay in my head.

The Nation's lost a granny
A lady quite renowned
There'll never be another
Even when our Charles is crowned.

No other Royal could meet her match
Her graciousness and poise.
Dignified and smiling,
Her silence made great noise.

A brave and stoic symbol,
A jewel and war queen,
Refusing to be sent away
From wartime London's scene.

Commoner not Royal,
Thrice asked to join the 'firm'
She stayed the course and raced it well.
Then saw it to full term.

She was the greatest Royal
This country's ever seen.
Visiting the homeless,
In the East End bombed out scene.

She match made for Diana!
Her one regret perhaps.
But thanks to her, another gem
Fell neatly in our laps.

Her passion was for horses
At home at race events.
No Gold Cup for her this year.
She's at the National's last fence.

Now at Westminster Abbey
She lies for state farewell.
One daughter gone, another left.
Grandchildren's tears won't quell.

Four pillars stand at corner stone
An evening vigil keep.
Thousands flock respectfully
To gaze, reflect and weep.

England's torment long forgotten
The trouble, death and strife.
Good people, free still 60 years
And she, a good King's wife.

My Favourite Goon

Today we lost a special goon.
At 82 he died too soon.
My Amy will never know the joy
Of such witty, clever, written ploy.

He always was somewhat insane
But his mania became our gain.
Creativity and a goon,
Combined for words that made us swoon.

Wide awake, he wrote at night,
Until he saw the first daylight.
He wrote and wrote, more and more.
Made us laugh til our ribs felt raw.

Distressed in mind, a cross to bear.
Life for some is never fair.
That someone troubled tortured through
Could make us laugh – me and you.

Ning, nang, nong and silly verse.
Output fired by manic curse.
Such a loss, his fun and wit.
We'll miss him more than just a bit.

We'll miss his tousled hair awry.
His jokes and twinkles from his eye.
We'll miss his humour, funny script.
Far too young, his life was nipped.

The Goons we'll listen on repeat
And giggle and wriggle in our seat.
So let's remember Spike for ever.
Forget the ning nang? Never, never.

A Simple Life
Written on the death of my mother-in-law in Oct 2002

A simple life.
No tangled web.
No jewels or riches.
No fame or celeb.

A pleasure to visit.
In window a wave.
To all who crossed threshold
Such pleasure you gave.

No large house or manse
But room in your heart
To keep others dear
Even if they're apart.

Your passing leaves sadness
An empty dull pain
And all that is left
Are the flowers we have lain.

But there's more when reflecting
On memories stored.
Sammy, Major and Ben
Dogs you adored.

The garden you sat in
Feeding birds from above.
Your flowers all thriving
From gold touch and love.

Puzzlebooks near the sweet tin.
On settee you curled.
Not much on TV!
All trouble in world!

Feelings are strange
On the M25,
Remembering visits,
When you were alive.

Now earth's door is closed
New window you'll view
While we journey forward
Remembering you.

So thank you, God bless you.
Over years you'd become
Much more than an in-law
My surrogate Mum.

What Happened

What happened to this life,
In rubbish tip, in bags?
A pack of Christmas paper,
Card boxes and some tags.

Some photos and a frame or two,
Showing happy faces.
Views and beaches, parks and walks
In all her favourite places.

A card reads, 'Mum we love you,
We'll be down Christmas Day!'
There's other cards with messages:
'You're 80! Happy Day!'

A Christmas list, names are crossed.
A few are marked 'deceased'.
Friends have gone, are sorely missed.
Grim Reaper's been a beast.

A silly hat, a blower too.
Some tinsel for the tree?
These remnants of a life well-lived
It could be you or me!

A starry decoration
Still folded in its pack.
No use this year as Santa Claus
Appears to have the sack.

A card to 'someone special'
Waiting for the pen.
For someone Christmas time this year
Will not be round again.

Hers and His

When he has gone, though sad and though blue
I'll do all things I have wanted to do!
I'll sing and play music; I'll wear what I like!
Won't cook, clean or shop but read books and just flop!
I'll paint up the house but first hold a rave!
I'll send to the charities naff presents he gave.
I'll hang up the pictures I bought at boot sales
And ignore those who say 'she's off the rails!'
I'll dump his mum's furniture and buy from Ikea
And do OU study on War and Crimea.

But it was silly of me to leave poems around
As he finished it on the day it was found.

'Now she has gone, I watch TV and sport!
I go to the cake shop for what she never bought!
I buy 'trashy' tabloids for page three and the scandal!
I don't do the garden – she'd call me a vandal!
I've thrown the naff jumpers she knitted for me!
And all those food items that were buy, get one free!
I go to the pub and come back *really* late!
I've wangled some help for the jobs that I hate!
I've dumped all the ornaments bought at boot sales!
Found room for my shirts on the wardrobe rails!'

But who was to blame for not heeding signs?
Perhaps they, like you, should have read 'tween the lines!

Marmalade

I always was a doggie peep.
I never thought of cats.
In fact, I thought my pussy friends
Were often raving bats!

They told me cats were clever,
Wily, full of wit!
Quite honestly, I thought their coos
Were just a load of…

Dogs come when called, I tried to say.
Oh yes, cats do that too!
And cats don't need to go for walks
The litter tray's for poo.

I never thought I'd have one,
But age came along, of course.
We thought we'd last forever,
A strident, walking force.

Less energy, less walking.
A dog was not for us.
But then we heard a little cat
Needed lots of fuss.

So when she came to live with me
I admit to feeling green.
I didn't understand this puss
Who acted like the Queen.

I didn't know that cats
Could be a step ahead.
She learned to know my thoughts
As they rattled through my head.

And now she's gone, the place is quiet
The chair is empty too.
The toys lay still, ignored and sad.
The basket waits... for who?

The Boomerang Generation

So here they come the once departed.
Home again and broken-hearted.
Three times more stuff than when they went
And all your money has been spent.

No more peace, can't be a slob!
Someone has to have a job.
Relaxing now is done at work
While empty-nesters sit and smirk.

Soon 'a while' expands to years.
Well-founded now the four-score fears.
Hoggin' phone and your computer,
You pray each day she finds a suitor.

Questioning your every move.
Ear-piercing music known as 'groove'.
First she's veggie. Then she's not.
Cannot eat the food you've got!

'Mum, just wondered…' and 'Perhaps…?'
Slowly all your strength she saps.
Money's short, a loan is needed.
All friends' warnings left unheeded.

'Tis not long before you muse,
Moving house could be a ruse?
Sell up and tell her 'that is that!'
'I'm moving to a one-bed flat!'

Denise A Horn.

Moving

From quickening in a mother's womb
To laying to rest in far off tomb.
What goes between is far from still.
Starting from birth and parents' thrill.

We move through childhood, can't wait to grow.
We break the rules, want to go,
To weave our way in God's wide world.
For teenage dreams to be unfurled.

To marry or to live in sin?
Whatever course, someone moves in!
From shifting sands to solid rock
Life has a way to move and mock.

At later stage a love may die.
One may move out – move one to cry.
Growing up midst toil and troubles.
Pleasure halves and heartache doubles.

But bigger moves are on the way.
A sudden thrust, a greater day!
That move to parenting is such
What went before won't matter much.

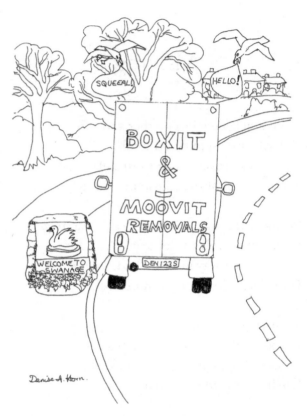

Then wee small eyes will move around
Til mother's form and breast is found.
Clutching, stretching, kicking, stalking
Rolling, crawling, standing, walking.

Then another's on the way
To stretch out father's meagre pay.
But somehow fate moves… never fear,
Promotion's here… move up a tier.

But now that house in which you rattled
Is filling fast with space embattled.
So off to agents with your needs
Exchanging old for brand new deeds.

But children come on short-term loan.
Discover soon they're home alone.
Then find they're strangers to each other
And run to arms of new found lover.

Some move to work, career and study.
Others find a soul mate buddy.
Some find one day that love's all gone.
Might wait a while and then move on.

And on the move they seek to find
Brand new partner of like mind!
Clubs and adverts. Points to prove?
Eye them up and make a move.

But love is strange and hard to test
And sometimes what you had was best
And when not looking it re-appears.
So now you're shedding happy tears!

Perhaps two families combine.
Some are his and some are mine.
More removal, relocation.
Exciting major operation!

Some moves are happy, some are sad.
Some are meant, enforced or mad!
Children leave, parents die.
Life moves too fast and time will fly.

And as we reach our autumn days
With slower limbs and brain in haze.
Soon every task becomes a chore.
Too soon comes death! We move no more!

Updating the Filofax

Out with the old,
In with the new.
Who knows, I might
Be deleting you.

Out with the names.
The dukes and the dames.
Out with work blighters.
In with the writers.

Out with those
Only wanting to nose.
In with the friends
There 'til the world ends.

The Filofax has a tale to tell
Of previous phases in a life lived well.
Labels and sellotape cannot disguise
Those blotted out for divorce or demise.

For the little book is laden
With near-forgotten contacts fading.
New pages added, stuck within
And I don't know where to begin.

Birthdays

Addresses

Calendar

Phone numbers

Appointments

Filo Fax

Gift lists

Denise A. Horn.

Anniversaries

Holidays

Guess Who?

Don't annoy a writer
Whatever else you do.
Don't make a comment or pull a face
Or she'll find a place for you!

She'll wrap you up in fancy clothes
And put you in her book,
Although you'll never realise,
Unless you take a look.

You will become a character
Who everyone will hate.
She'll make your lover spurn you
After going for a date.

No, don't annoy a writer.
She's watching every move.
She sits there people watching,
As her pen is soon to prove.

No don't annoy a writer.
Don't be grumpy, curt or rude.
Don't stress her or harass her
Or start a family feud.

No don't annoy a writer.
Her notebook records it all.
Every thought and news you told her
Will be used to bring your fall.

No, don't annoy a writer.
Just stay her bestie friend
And then you'll be the character
Who has a happy end.

Denise A. Horn.

Index of First Lines

Acknowledgements

A big thank you to all those who took the trouble to let me know how much they enjoyed *Grandma's Poetry Book* as this gave me the confidence and inspiration to compile the more general poems I have written over the years into this collection. Denise has, once again, provided fabulous illustrations and pointed out where poems were not finished or did not sound right. All this is much appreciated. In fact, without her I would not have such lovely books.

I remain indebted to Roderick Grant for reading through the initial draft of my first book and for encouraging me along the journey that has been the promotion of 'Grandma'.

I would also like to thank the following bookshops and emporiums which have stocked Grandma's Poetry Book and have also expressed interest in stocking this second book. New and Secondhand Books, Station Road, Swanage, Candleworld, High Street, Swanage, The Old Stables (emporium), particularly Kevin and Julie who have been such a support over the last two years, especially helping two novices put up a gazebo in a strong wind. Thanks also go to Gulliver's Bookshop, Wimborne, The Westbourne Bookshop, Winstone's in Sherborne, The Bridport Bookshop, Good Books in Bridport who let me do regular book signings, Wardon Hill Trading Post on the Yeovil Road (A37), Birdcage Barn emporium in Birdham, East Sussex, The Little Gallery in the Courtyard Craft Centre in Lytchett Minster, The Little Blue Emporium at the Orchard Garden Centre, Gillingham, Dorset, 4EverVintage, Blandford, Wareham Tourist Information Centre, and, most recently, Ruth, at the Purbeck Artisan Yard, Wareham, for recognising the potential of *Grandma's Poetry Book*.

A tongue in the cheek thank you to all the people I have observed over the years, at work, socially and while sitting in the sun on the beach and the snippets I have overheard on buses and trains which led me to put pen to paper. I must also mention the national press and TV news programmes which provide a hive of ideas and amusement.

Last but not least, I am grateful to all my family and friends who have inadvertently provided ideas, conversations and experiences which may have triggered a rhyme but, more importantly provide me with much love, fun and support.

Di Castle

Di Castle was born and bred in Hertfordshire. She always had a love of words and started writing as soon as she could hold a pen. After her youngest daughter went to school she began a career teaching in Further Education, while collecting a hoard of unfinished manuscripts. She began writing poems more seriously on her move to Swanage. Later, her writing took precedence and, since becoming a regular attendee at the Winchester Writers' Conference, she has enjoyed success in their competitions gaining two first prizes and highly commended for articles on a range of subjects.

In the 1980s, Di was one of the prominent writers for the Terry Wogan morning show on Radio 2 with around one hundred letters read out on air. She now writes for websites including www.henpicked.net www.oapschat. co.uk and for Depression Alliance and has articles published on Gransnet.

Di enjoyed a nomadic existence in Oxfordshire, Hertfordshire, Middlesex and South Bucks before finally settling in Swanage in 2001. She lives close to her partner, Bryan, in a Victorian building overlooking Swanage Bay with views to Bournemouth and Old Harry Rocks. She has three daughters and seven grandchildren.

Her debut, Grandma's Poetry Book, was published in 2014.

Should I Wear Floral? And Other Poems on Life, Love and Leaving, is her second poetry book.

Denise Horn

Denise Horn was born and bred in Yorkshire. As a child she always loved drawing and this continued into her teens, when she studied Art at the College of Ripon & York St. John. From there she went on to teach young children and enjoyed bringing the world of Art into their lives, enriching their art lessons by introducing mixed media and building their confidence in producing art work of a high standard. Denise moved from Yorkshire to Northampton when she married, and started a family, eventually moving to Swanage, Dorset, where she became a part of the large artist community. As a member of The Arts Club, she exhibits her bright, highly detailed paintings of the local area regularly.

Grandma's Poetry Book was her first venture into serious illustration work.

Denise takes commissions for her art work. See her Facebook page: https://www.facebook.com/DenzArt123/?fref=ts

She can also be contacted: via www.dicastle.co.uk